1970

EAST
BY
SOUTHWEST

POEMS BY

NEIL
CLAREMON

SIMON AND SCHUSTER
NEW YORK

First printing

SBN 671–20542–0 Cloth
SBN 671–20602–8 Paper
Library of Congress Catalog Card Number: 78–107249
Designed by Edith Fowler
Manufactured in the United States of America
by H. Wolff Book Mfg. Co., Inc., New York

FOR JUDITH, MY WIFE

CONTENTS

*But still for us existence is enchanted: from a hundred
   places
it is still origin. A play of pure forces
that no one touches unless he kneels and admires.*

Rilke: To Orpheus II. 10
translated by C. F. MacIntyre

THIS OTHER TIDE

SHARK

Smelling of the sea, a scavenger
image whose wake is the bonetrail
drapes over the trawlers.

It hangs, a white hide
and blood bringing black flies
to crawl over rows of teeth.

Its size attracts attention
of those on the wharf who
marvel at the depths.

Black globular eyes
bulge in the sun
to know creatures of metal.

But the crowd is its catch;
a lure, it rises on a line
into a sky of blue coral.

When it flashes again
the crowd turns to mackerel;
my hands drop the reel.

SQUALL

The sea foams in the harness
of the hidden moon, rain
drums steadily on a tin
gutter as I read
                    Poe's words
piercing like spindle-back chairs,
his storm-dark past thumbing
thru my brain in the designs
on the rain-washed windows
                              kicking up
my suspicion of the leaf
stick figures along
the washed out path
                    as I am
and afraid for his world
to be on the edge
of this unreeling night.

                    I would sleep
but my head's so clogged
the pressure of the blood
                              breathes
loudly against my breathing
like another
                and a beacon
from the lighthouse of the sheriff
pinwheels in the rain
                    as I watch
the window, not knowing what
might tap on the pane, arrest
this other tide.

THE VISITOR

His footstep is light, leaving
no path in the yard; can
be heard if quiet's
the mood heart
invites in . . . though he is
shy and will vanish
at call of his name
he has come
                I have thought him there
while nailing up fences
in the moist sun; a dark suit
in a crowd
listening to music
I have heard him
as a story, as a warning
to get off
or onto the stage . . . he speaks to me
often of my shame
                    yet he has come
like a slave
at night when the rain is cold,
to my bidding when others regret
the sight of my face—
sometimes drunk, noisy, climbing
my back, sometimes with grace
in his rhythm
                but for a time
he has walked past the yard
leaving prints
illegible in the dust, beginning
abruptly and disappearing
as fast
          wherever he is
he comes for me
when the setting sun puts
a light show of shadow
on the mountains, when musicians
too tired to care
play tales of sound
their own lives

15

to the pelt-adorned crowd; this
I have spoken of
at other hours, laughing
and said it was the abominable
snowman who comes
                    but he is more
foreign than that.

SUBURBAN PRESERVE

Out of the acre wood
simple snow on leafless
branches, white sound
and on the ground, tracks
of a squirrel; they
tell the whole
thru the suburban preserve,
men treasure seeking,
children lost of the magic way
wood of the witch's charm,
it's a wonder who
shall find it again as
I come to the portico
and fumble for the keys
to the door where once
my house stood behind
but now in blank snow
is no longer there;
the nurse no longer reading
how in the end everyone
lived happily with kids
had ever after who grew
to prince and princesshood
or to toads and hags
but then were kissed
while I have lost the key
it seems, besides
the house is gone—
what would you say
shut out of the damn
once upon a place house
but that I have lost
the way in a storm
looking for something
strangely happy shouting
wild to the utterly sane
though I begin to pause
at my door, in a rage
locked inside and out.

NOTHING IS FAMILIAR HERE

Nothing is familiar here
in this room I grew up in,
the color scheme has changed
the wall map is outdated,
my feet overstraddle
the old mattress, and drawers
are full of things I don't
recall, except there is
the single width of bed
the sleep of my parents,
of lovers who have had
their children; I long
for the odor you've worn
down your cleavage
to enter this uneven square,
for you to tussle with me
in this blueberry dark
where we shall become
singers of a fluid form.

PLASTICS

The novocain numbs and swells
the pâté of brain against the skull
dulling the surgical incision
and heavy tapping at the bone.

My eyes know all they wish to
of the dazzling whitewash
beneath the hospital lamps
in the heat of their own dark.

The scalpel's probings carve out
the reeling circles from which
I came, for years drifting in
the convex images of my mind.

I've come to please the blondes
with brittle faces and wake to see
how my face has been blackened,
distorted and held by a gauze mask.

Looking in the polished mirror,
when the doctor returns I am
hardly able to ask
if I will ever assimilate.

DIALOGUE

"Remember

in the White Mountains

near Show Low

a stream

they had stocked

where you fished

day and night

catching nothing

and never spoke

or laid me, we

almost parted."

"I see now

yearlings from the lodge

too young to ride

that ran on a small hill

above the stream

at dusk each night

but one evening

were encircled by a full

pale moon in which

they did somersaults

and in the dawn

vanished as we left."

PHILOSOPHER'S STONE

Take the spray of light
as sun passes thru the dust
and dress the sovereign bride
in its gentle tone, then
deck the husband out in tincture
of sulphur afire and stand them
on the running water to be joined
by an alchemist in gold while
the guests gather strands of stone
to tie the marriage knot round
the vessel of their bones; let her
take his spirit to find him
mineral and herb, let him take
her soul to forage in the dark
for they from the moisture
of the red grape must make
their love stone yield silver
to detain a ray of light.

RIPENING OF THE APPLES

Of the many apple trees—
red fruit set tentatively
against the blue, the crop
is much sparer than before:
an autumn in 1966, heaving
with apples—our home less
awkward in the orchard's wake.

I was thankful for the apples,
for the raking of leaves,
once with one car and no TV;
each visitor brought some gadget
to help in our first harvest.

This orchard is dying,
the city spreading,
trucks shifting thru nights
I'd lie watching a fog
put the house to sleep.

On the ground each sweet-
rotting core's world is unsure
tho none will spawn trees.

TO HEISENBERG
FOR PROOF OF UNCERTAINTY

Our cat is lost, the one
with an individual bent;
her tears pace the floor,
each bush is camouflage,
I swear I shut the door
yet her fingers grow claws,
time spins slower; she says
my life's an alibi, leaning
on despair is sure I left
the latch open while staring
at a star, but I never budged
lodged in the night, so
she must have let the cat out
in a wailing dream where
the moon drowns in the sea;
still, the cat is lost
and it's hard to know
whose dreams belong to whom
no less where the cat is.

MAYAKOVSKY

Across the tundra, heartbeats
leave imprints, a drum
undying calls
for another revolution
to be reborn,
nothing astir
but bones of words
ignored—I
had been anxious
for the marketplace
and now in the clamor
of verbose crowds
have come to love
a married woman
my anarchy; comrade
our twin lands
talk of suicide
but I haven't the swagger
to get up and die.

CLEARING

It's not winter,
we can lie in the fields,
the pastures of derelict barns
and tractors long rusting
into manure.

I watch the flakes
drop off and seek asylum
in the sandy soil.

You ask what rains
will spoil aluminum
and stainless steel?

A sagging gate points,
a broken weather vane
whirls like a police light;

the grass grows thru our bones—

We have left many things behind
to be alone.

STRANGE PEAKS

TIME TO KILL

1.
Looking for someone to take me on
I walk slow
as the growing agave—
the yucca blades
in morning shadows
cutting the highway
that runs thru a swelter of sand.

2.
At midday near the border,
Nogales whores
turn up a dirt road hugged
by 2-story bars, wearing
trinkets of their conquistadores.

3.
By the San Xavier mission
vesper bells
call the Papagos
from the charity gardens;
hired hands, in ignorance they
camouflage missile sites for SAC.

4.
On muted tires
the cars curve drunkenly down the road
while pastels of sunset carouse.

5.
At home a Sabbath candle is burning.

BABOQUIVARI

Moving up the slopes to thickets
of manzanita, the air is cool
and lighter, sparrows are singing.

In the valley waves of green
and the foam of white rocks
wash against distant hills.

Other ranges move slowly south
like icebergs; shadows of clouds
find paths on the bowl of earth.

This is as high as I need go;
darkness will bring the puma's cry
and strange peaks of a queer planet,

Then headlights along the road
to Kitt Peak where our scientists
have established another outpost.

WESTERN PROVINCIAL

The hunter shoulders his rifle and walks
into the endless hills after the lion
crazed by a bullet who crosses the land;
over scorched mesas he walks as he trails
the beast down from its lair to the river
on the lowland where deer and cattle graze.

Above, rising toward its red noon, the sun
arcs so slowly it seems to circle around
like a hawk—the brushwood seems to spread
like fire while the spider, snake, or scorpion
wait in shadows and a small man with rag props
in his boots hurls stones at two young girls.

To the west Kennedy is dead, to the east
the Reverend King is shot; thru swollen eyes
he sees life and land at war in the scarcity
of green yet blended so in the desert terrain
he cannot see the cat for the arbor of thorn.

America's choir lifts its voice to the sky,
a deer leaps from the brush, the cat behind;
his head whips with the crack of a backbone's
snapping and he aims at the blood-soaked bodies
moving in a cycle of rock, sand, tooth and claw.

ELEMENTS I–XVI

I

Halo shattered with sweat
my body bakes, muscles
clamped, mouth
craving saliva;
in this breathless heat
I tread water (appreciation
for the use of a hacienda
in Casa Grande in July)

Windows open
the inner courtyard—there
stone is too hot for walking on,
in the shade of banana leaves
the fruit is limp;
I can hear the ants
pass a sleeping lizard,
on his back
the air weighs a ton.

If she'd return I would go down
to drink from her.

II

Outside
the growing sun
makes rocks glitter
glow red
shimmer into puddles,
a car melts to a pool
of tin;
the servants are cross,
nothing works.

Dust whirls in the wind
clatters against the glass;
a dryness can be heard
it seeps into me,
not even gin cures.

My skin is tough
as a cactus hide,
I will write of nymphs
naked in the water;
unable, slowly I drift
out on the weather,
it holds me.

III

At five P.M. rain
washes the dust
from the air, polishing
the stones and plants;
a perfume, creosote,
clasps the body,
thru a crystal sheen
I see the needle-
points of cactus
glisten like ice.

Breathing, I forget
the life of others,
see hundreds of miles;
with each turn create
mountains, inside
a flash flood
speeds thru the riverbed,
catches trucks that kill
furry things and over-
turns them.

IV

On the night air
I hear the javelina,
the jaguar,
the diamondback
racing to meet
the girl with soft eyes
who talks to them.

If she'd return?

she, who will not breathe
the diesel air of men,
naked as she runs,
breasts full—thighs
parting to a new moon;
men who spy her
are turned to deer.

I lope off into a field.

V

Wild stallion
voice off the far hills
after a mare,
    (I hear your call, listening
    above the sahuaro
    and ocotillo
    as a searchlight
    from the air base
    shoots at stars
    leaving tufts of white clouds.)

Long after the barrage, a pinto,
sighing, entices only shadows
in a false dawn; his silences
so clear I feel oceans of patience
foaming into madness.

VI

Near Scottsdale, Mexicans
picked half the pima cotton
before falling of sunstroke,
their tanned bodies lie now
fleeced in white fibers;
they are speechless.
On beaches somewhere in Asia
far from their missions
machine-gunned men lie
buried in equipment.

I have seen his mate,
she has
powerful haunches
but stumbles crossing
shell craters
in New Mexico.

36

VII

Slower than usual, my
branches tuned by the wind
shade graves growing moss;
the cool feeling relaxes,
roots sinking down to mingle
with bones of cliff dwellers
who raised corn
in this desert.

When sun peaks in Yuma
there is nothing to do,
tho I would flow
in a heat rising
like water swirling
in a wind at Mazatlán,
for when body is calmed
the mind walks on water,
not out of the thirst
known when the barrel cactus
is dry, but from looking
too long

at the perfectly still.

VIII

A last red flame ignites
in the sky,
day's last mood wanes,
the eye squints,
a gray cloud, the final light
settles;
out of their clods of soil
the longhorn beetles emerge
to tread on the unshut eye.

To think of the body
still when the rot of it
sinks into the vine
that twists out of its root,

a cemetery jammed
with spires and squares
as a city that mocks
the skyline,

one corpse undiscovered
in Sonora—even
the marrow dries.

IX

One rides afield, desert birds
he cannot name scream
as they hunt the foothills; these
shrieks of a desert burial
follow him as thoughts
of a public funeral, as
routes taken from intensive
care units, calling
from some bitter pride
to be quietly separate,
a white skull unmoved.

By dawn the morsels
will be gone, buzzards must tear
thru clothing for liver and heart,
the sun starts its cremation.

Accelerating, wheels barely
touch the road, telephone poles
a long fence; on a cycle
this is the highway
year '69, storms
of gnats clog the nostrils,
hands rise from the handlebars.

X

Cats smeared into the pavement,
dogs bloody by the roadside,
to be removed; Utah
time and the dead sea,
races of people insensitive
to salt, torn, floating
bellies to the gulls.

Salt rubbed in the wounds,
spirit robed in humidity
walking in the trail of the body,
past its deserted homes.

Arrival; the coyotes
gorged reach the salt lick,
a doe,
my mistress, runs off,
I turn whimpering
back into earth.

The plain verse of the Seventies begins.

XI

A shrike singing a mockingbird's song
waits to hang its prey
on a sahuaro arm,
mesquites' bare limbs
waver dark as charred trees,

he kills for pleasure.

XII

Standing upright
like one-legged men
sahuaros wait the night
so dark Earth can't face
the moon, when an army
might slip down
from the hills
and overrun our kind.

In the dusk the land seems
more alive as if herds
of silent creatures stampeded
fearing the red fire lapping
over the mountain peaks,
the glow—a lantern
above my newspaper.

I read
at a hospital doctors found
a child had seven bones broken,
his father too drunk
to make a statement.

XIII

In the New World I have caught scurvy
and lain at the porthole watching
the white ghost ship laden
with South American fruit.

In the corridors of the recovery room
the alcohol tires me,
I see gila monsters baking
on red rocks and wish
to sleep the break of hibernation.

Sleepless, I watch the ironwoods
across the way; will they know how
to shield the children I fathered
with my sight? I, all bone, seeing
children raised like cattle
herded left–right
thru the stockyards
in the heat by the pits.

Phoenix rousing in the smog.

XIV

When the ground first hardened
the flatness stirred something to spires;
using boulders
two pillars
were set skyward
marking the western shore;
later, the earth cracked
mountains heaved from the sea,
they fell
toppling in a ring of rocks
balanced on rocks; then
the Benson highway parted them,
yet dawn, the first campfire,
lights figures dancing
in worship of the spire maker.

Driving thru, each time
I look for him.

XV

In the skull a blue sky
so blue the sage is yellow,
the sun looms whitely
shedding purple clouds;
moon a glazed eye
mountains appearing
like a Cyclops under it—
four jackrabbits drop
down their holes,
day opens up,
something moves.

Where nothing seemed
another boulder
on the fringe
of a red sandstone town
crept into the desert.

XVI

Not another human wakes for a hundred miles
out of solitude
space tired of its blankness
begins matter
and it fissions;
at times
you can hear the change-over.

In the Arizona desert
watching crawling things
clean the night's dead
I think of a world
endlessly
devouring itself.

Under a golden sky
something is dying,
a priest comforts the indifferent
with another world,
an ignorant animal
unable to see or hear
crawls thru this one;
I think

the rocks are crying.

SONOITA

An Arab stallion dapple
in his wild colthood,
a schoolgirl holding
to the silver mane,
canter from their stable
in spray of trodden soil.

Effortlessly they sail across
the shorn foothills, turning
the earth's corner, headed
for an oasis in a land
where all is horses,
bridles hang upon the palms.

Tired, her mother waits
by adobe stalls
shy of words to calm
her apprehension; she has
known the gait of passion
and fears the wild herds.

Like an old hired hand
she waits in shadows
for the child who riding
unbroken in the saddle
heeds not the love of men
but lives bejeweled
where there are none.

JUNCTION

How far into our bodies our hands delve
to follow the course of love; a buzzard
hovering a dark cloud at the red summit
as we come to the curve on the trail,
wiping the sweat sun drew to our brow.

Peak towering ferrous to the jagged eye
with swift strokes of the brush levels
the ravine to an easel it draws us on,
and the rattler—head arched as the peak;
heat dropping hard on a 60-mile silence.

What fate the shadow of a thorn casts
over our pounds of flesh planted before
the smooth curves of the serpent while
the sun passes four in the afternoon;
our leather soles worn to each stone.

On a single fold of the canvas we stand
reduced to large horseflies—delving
as toxic venom held in the snake's fangs
freezes our body; the time passing into
coiled, red peaks shut in its eye slits.

FIGURES

I

Long fingers of the wind
gather the fine dust
to wrap night in its veil,
and the pale moon rotates
slowly, looming large, not far
on its journey from the sea;
what items man leaves behind,
his rusting tools sanded by winds
left molten in a mercurial light,
his wooden sheds turned ashen
by the sun to gleam in the dark,
are scattered shells that reveal
the fleshy oyster has been eaten,
the few drops of pearl extracted;
are merged to a striated rainbow
of metal veins in the slag heap
falling with silver and gold dust
into the copper pit in the hill.

II

Where the rotted agave's clear tequila
serves as lubricant or antiseptic—
the dark eyes of the lithe ones
who keep their families in the hills;
one, standing at a bar window
night rouge blending to rich skin
set off in orange lace against black hair
and fine Castillian features,
fixes the walker in the street
with cold onyx Indian eyes
knowing in their twenties
(as if the window-mirrored street
framed an artist's masterpiece)
life's inner strain, and the color
white for martyrs and virgins.

III

On the Sitgreaves Pass road,
once the mountain route of 66,
to rest in a gutted hotel
after the wind and the road
have burned into the face,
and sleep under a ceiling
covered with clouds in shadow
of the high arch that was
an entrance to the 3 corners
left standing, lets suspicion
close over and the sliding stones
during the moon's sudden flash
thru a spreading white mist
strain the muscles of sleep,
till morning when the sun
silhouettes a ghost town,
striking a red stone slab
in the center of the room
to bring back the priest
druid or Aztec, and sense
of a cold, purple bloodstone
clutched in the right hand.

IV

From the fire, a yolk;
layers of glutinous rock;
then shell perfectly stressed
but ever so thin to ride on,
and if there is a natural fault
it is in the man riding
to where the pavement ends
on Canal St. in the Sonoran desert;
his monstrous earth digger
provided by Anaconda
can only scratch the surface,
his fifty dollars will not buy
the sacrificial lamb,
and if it does—the knife
leaves no visible scar,
little blood is lost
on the soft altar, but then
again the thin membrane
will never heal to the shell.

OLD NEGATIVES

BALANCES

I

You are the man;
                        you have
seen the seasons change round
the hem of the years,
too often at seven-twenty
woken to the alarm of her body,
the same old spider
black midpoint of the clock
set on the ivory face
of her flesh, longing
for another.
And found another
bathing on the terrace, her fresh
beauty rivaling the sun,
crossed her legs with yours
rushed the sequence of events
tense in the lights
of dazed eyes.
And woke
spilled out of yourself
to find some excuse
to call the hour late, left
caught in the unordained
moment of your lust, the child
within withering
till it dies;
                        have you
gone round the circle of love
and hate, knowing
                        there are
no prayers for the future?

II

The fan blows branches
back to their trees
as I spiral
in the busy patterns
of leaves on a rug,
and a child wails
in a nearby house;
                having
shot a loud robin
as a tin can,
it lay a flutter
of wings;

when I came near
small talons threatened
as I left
an orange breast
soaked itself in red,
two eyes closed;

on higher ground
an eagle dove
for a newborn lamb
and rose in shrieks
to cross a rifle shot
that dropped it
shredding entrails
from its prey.

When I woke, from somewhere
a prophet, or clap
of thunder, said
"Thou shalt not build the house."

PASSINGS

From the raw meat
dripping,
swathed in fat and
cut to quarters,
the animal reduced to pounds
a lamb, a calf, a cow
on racks—the metal hooks
thru sides of flesh
in the *traife* shop or
meat market for the wholesaling
of life's guts;

     from two men,
two men come in the ship's hold
without fineness of the word
or easy hours, there came
from old negatives and sepia tones
a family,
   dimly
in its memory
splattered aprons.

Now after their passing,
a passing,
   a dry cleaning
hands washed clean
of grease,
   grass
flowers
far as the eye sees;
out of a brick-stained city
buildings,
deeds, land, investments
in Mexico in fish,
in the processing
     of pink flesh;
the heads sliced away
from afar
without the casualty
of a world's fingers
dripping in blood.

CROWDS

Terrace bars rise now,
tho not so high as the steeple
above the marchers
on the avenue,
Victory day, Hitler
lying in a pool of blood,
                    a small pool
the worst yet to come
                    the pits,
and maggots on the bodies
packed by bulldozers,
                              gas
exuding from uncovered graves
dissipating in the air
                    that now
with the finding of a woman
who cut nipples of Jewesses
at Buchenwald, we hear
from the street
                    she was
a good neighbor,
"who remembers Buchenwald?"
such deaths legend,
the ovens, mythlike—
                    bombs
blazing above Hanoi
no more real
in the traffic jam,
                    marchers
who remember, who can see
death as the pain in their cells
lying in the streets
                    clubbed
gashes in their heads, billy clubs
waving in the air,
                         eyes closing
in the color of television
to this sight, sounds of politicos
afraid of the crowds, the pressure
of bodies moving against silk suits.

Behind him
the living room fills with suits
thru the grated doors he sees drinks
ease the tongues of the celebrants
hearing the news from Germany;
                          he is scared
of things so large yet ogles
when the parents are gone
and the German boyfriend
slides his hand up the thighs
of the maid before the menorah.

                    Everything is larger
than himself; in crowds at the circus
he wants to sit on the elephants
to see eye to eye with monsters
shouting, extending hands, fists
clenched behind their backs:

                    as he is lost;
later, his sister was lost
the trees and thickets around him
his sister crying, Central Park
circling him—huge buildings
to peer thru their glass;
he calls out for God, the God
claimed when the self is too small
and won't do;
                    in his fear
thoughts push each other aside;
hearing the shots, or backfires
he wishes to be a crowd.

INTERSECTIONS

Old man your bride
deceives you

she lies serene her arms around
the burning child, bullet
in her head, a yellow epitaph
to this Christmas card . . .
she rises
weary
from the cold December ground
runs a comb thru her matted hair
and disappears to mend her mind
in cover of the reeds

my wife turns pale, nauseous
searches her womb
for her art against those
who die
            innocent
spreads the skirts above her knees
reclining
brush of thighs in the reed
waiting
crush of her lover

Messiah
I pity you, if you come
down here; it's not the view
but nowhere is an immaculate
mother to be found;
crosses
not just nails and swords
but burning

her lover in kerosene sits
meditating on the match

in Palestine, along the Jordan

the cradle of civilization
rocks

she clutches
her womb, hot
with the seed of God
wings of the angel fading
into the sky, hope
in the child no man
would beget
on the bullet-ridden field,

a voice

from the womb

calling out

to the old man, the
illegitimate Father

RUBICON

The train
from the tail of my memory
careens
      thru the night fields
south
to the peg leg of America
Florida
      buried somewhere
in the swamps
      the fountain of youth.

a boy still trying
to grow into his face
clasps a mother's hand
on the station platform

he is aware of the cop
wearing rule on his hip,
the silver of his pistol
teasing the clasped hand.

hand clasped as now
I hold yours
teasing
      dawn
at dawn
the boy leaps
to the coupling
between the cars
where Negro porters
take on oranges
      as the train
slowly moves out
swerving
bouncing
rhythmic under his body

      transport as a woman.

in the woodpen yards
young girls squat
facing the tracks
with squalor
                allure
                of the limbs
the suit
of wool
he wears
scouring
his thighs
as he sits
erect in rooms of adults.

this train
bears sailors
past Pensacola
to Korea,
taking their last leer
at the women
aware of the jogging motion
the Pullman makes
carrying sweet aromas
of orange peels.

he was meant to be
saccharine
his girls
were meant
to have pedigree
his first girl
had pinkpants
she said, boys
tickle; at Fort Lauderdale
Sunday '53
the weather is shut thighs.

        the train speeds to its destination
        an orange blossom special
        in Ponce de León's nightmare
        a vibration

A harsh, lyrical quality pervades these poems set within the stark, shimmering desert terrain of Arizona and New Mexico. In that surreal landscape where giant boulders jut like "strange peaks of a queer planet," where Daliesque images melt into memory, where event and emotion become fused "from looking too long/at the perfectly still," Claremon breaks through the sensuous immediacy of the searing heat to recall a different kind of desolation: coming of age in the urban and suburban preserves of the East Coast where he was born. *East by Southwest*, which marks the debut of a 26-year-old poet, routes us in a unique direction across two regions of the American scene.